THIS BOOK BELONGS TO:

ONCE THERE WAS A

Gigi and Papa

WHO WANTED
A LITTLE ONE,
JUST LIKE YOU!

THE DAY YOU ARRIVED
THEY CRIED TEARS OF JOY,
YOU WERE BEAUTIFULLY BRAND NEW!

Their love for you is a treasure,
that no one can take away.

Gigi and Papa

WILL HOLD YOU CLOSE IN THEIR HEARTS,

EACH AND EVERY DAY.

Your beautiful face brightens up the darkest of nights!

WATCHING YOU LEARN AND GROW
IS THEIR FAVORITE SIGHT.

THEY LOVE TO PLAY
WITH YOU, AND TELL
YOU STORIES TOO!

Gigi and Papa

LOVE TO WATCH YOU GROW AND LEARN,

IN ALL YOU DO.

THEY CHERISH
EVERY MOMENT,
FROM DAWN TILL
SETTING SUN.

THEIR LOVE FOR YOU,
LITTLE ONE, WILL
NEVER BE OUTDONE.

They'll always be there
to comfort you,
when you're feeling blue.

Gigi and Papa

WILL BE THERE TO CELEBRATE,

ALL THE NEW THINGS YOU CAN DO.

They love to laugh and giggle, and listen when you talk.

AND THEY'RE THERE TO LEND A HAND,
WHEN YOU WANT TO GO FOR A WALK.

SO HOLD THEIR HANDS, NEVER LET GO.

PLEASE KNOW THAT THEIR LOVE,
WILL CONTINUE TO GROW.

They love you more than you could ever know!

Made in the USA
Monee, IL
25 November 2024

71194045R00021